Ponce de León

Discover The Life Of An Explorer

Trish Kline

Rourke Publishing LLC
Vero Beach, Florida 32964

PHOTO CREDITS:
©Archive Photos: cover, title page, pages 15, 18, 21; ©Andre Jenny/Focus
Group: page 4; ©James P. Rowan: pages 7, 9, 12; ©Getty Images: page 10;
©Artviile LLC: page 13; Library of Congress: page 17

EDITORIAL SERVICES:
Pamela Schroeder

Library of Congress Cataloging-in-Publication Data

Kline, Trish.
    Ponce de León / Trish Kline.
      p. cm. — (Discover the life of an explorer)
    Includes bibliographical references and index.
    ISBN 1-58952-068-8
    1. Ponce de Leân, Juan, 1460? - 1521—Juvenile literature. 2. Explorers—
America—Biography—Juvenile literature. 3. Explorers—Spain—Biography—
Juvenile literature. 4. America—Discovery and exploration—Spanish—
Juvenile literature. [1. Ponce de Leân, Juan, 1460?-1521. 2. Explorers. 3.
America—Discovery and exploration—Spanish.] I. Title.

E125.P7 .K58 2001
972.9'02'092—dc21
  [B]   2001019003

Printed in the USA

TABLE OF CONTENTS

FROM ROYAL COURT TO BATTLE

Don Juan Ponce de León was a Spanish **explorer**. He was born around 1460. He lived in the country of Spain. As a boy, Ponce de León worked as a **messenger** in the royal court. Later he trained as a soldier and fought in many battles. Ponce de León lived during a time of great discoveries. Many explorers were sailing to lands far away. When they returned home, they were called heroes. Ponce de León wanted to be a hero, too.

Ponce de León was a great explorer.

SAILING WITH CHRISTOPHER COLUMBUS

In 1492 Christopher Columbus discovered the New World. He returned to Spain with the news. The king and queen of Spain gave Columbus ships and sailors for the trip. Ponce de León was one of the sailors. Columbus set sail again in 1493.

During his travels Columbus discovered many islands. When he returned to Spain, Ponce de León stayed behind on one of the islands. Today this island is known as the Dominican Republic.

Christopher Columbus discovered the New World.

GOLD!

In 1508 Ponce de León learned that gold had been found. It was on a nearby island. Today the island is known as Puerto Rico. Ponce de León went to the island. In 1509 he took **settlers** there. The settlement was near the modern-day city of San Juan. The King of Spain was happy. Ponce de León had found both land and gold for Spain. The king named Ponce de León the governor of the new land.

Ponce de León lived in this home in Puerto Rico.

JUAN PONCE DE LEON,

SEARCHING FOR THE FOUNTAIN OF YOUTH.

FOUNTAIN OF YOUTH

Ponce de León heard stories from the Native Americans about a "**Fountain** of Youth." They said that the waters of the fountain had the power to make a person young again. They also said that much gold lay around the fountain.

Ponce de León told the king of Spain about this fountain. The king gave him ships and men. In 1513 Ponce de León began his search for the Fountain of Youth.

Ponce de León wanted to find the fountain of youth.

A fort in Saint Augustine stands where Ponce de León first set foot in Florida.

Ponce de León sailed from Puerto Rico to the Florida coast.

THE PLACE OF FLOWERS

Ponce de León sailed north from Puerto Rico. He searched for the island the Native Americans described. He did not find the Fountain of Youth. Instead, Ponce de León found a new land. This land had many, many flowers.

Ponce de León named the new land Pascua Florida, the place of flowers. He claimed it in the name of the king of Spain. Today it is known as the state of Florida.

Florida was claimed for the king of Spain.

A POISONED ARROW

In the place of flowers, the Native Americans were not friendly. They wanted the strangers to leave. The Native Americans attacked Ponce de León and his men. Ponce de León escaped to his ship.

Eight years later, in the winter of 1521, Ponce de León returned to the land of flowers. He took 500 men with him. He hoped to settle a colony. He soon found out that he had chosen a bad place to settle.

Ponce de León returned to the land of flowers in 1521.

There was little food or fresh water. Ponce de León led men into a forest, hoping to find a river. What he found were unfriendly Native American warriors. Ponce de León was shot with a **poisoned** arrow. The soldiers carried Ponce de León to his ship where he soon died.

Ponce de León died from a poisoned arrow.

BONES OF A LION

Juan Ponce de León never found the Fountain of Youth. Instead, his search led him to find new lands. After he discovered the land of flowers, other explorers followed. Soon settlers followed, too.

When he died in February, 1521, Ponce de León was buried under the **altar** inside a church. On his **gravestone** was written, "Below lay the bones of a lion."

Menendez built a colony in the land of flowers after Ponce de León died.

IMPORTANT DATES TO REMEMBER

1460	Juan Ponce de León was born.
1493	Sailed to the New World with Christopher Columbus.
1509	Took settlers to Puerto Rico. Served as governor until 1512.
1513	Left Puerto Rico to search for the Fountain of Youth. Landed in Florida and claimed it for the king of Spain.
1521	Wounded by poisoned arrow and later died.

GLOSSARY

altar (OL ter) — table-like platform used in religious services

explorer (ik SPLOR er) — someone who travels to unknown places

fountain (FOWN ten) — a structure water flows from

gravestone (GRAYV stohn) — a stone that marks a grave

messenger (MES en jer) — a person who delivers messages

poisoned (POY zend) — something that can cause illness or death when swallowed, breathed in, or rubbed on skin

settlers (SET el erz) — people who made homes in new territories

INDEX

Further Reading

Manning, Ruth. *Juan Ponce de León.* Heinemann Library, 2000.
O'Brien, Patrick. *The Ponce de León.* Raintree Steck-Vaughn, 2000.

Websites To Visit

encarta.msn.com
www.gale.com
www.floridahistory.org

About The Author

Trish Kline is a seasoned curriculum writer. She has written a great number of nonfiction books for the school and library market. Her print publishing credits include two dozen books as well as hundreds of newspaper and magazine articles, anthologies, short stories, poetry, and plays. She currently resides in Helena, Montana.